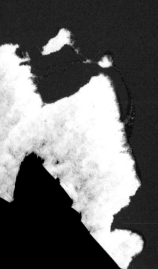

EXPLORING HISTORY

JAPAN

RICHARD TAMES

Belitha Press
In association with the Royal Geographical Society

Foreword

Previous page: A pond in one of the earliest Zen gardens in Kyoto. The torii gateway in the foreground is a Shinto motif.

This page: The Shinto god of Hell holding a scroll.

Many animals, birds and fish regularly travel over great distances. What sets people apart is the ability to explore and discover. An explorer is someone who is curious about the world and if you are curious enough to read this book then you too have become an explorer.

Exploring is not just about boarding a plane or sailing a boat to a place you have never been before – you have to record what you see, listen to the people you meet and learn about the place you find. This book follows in the footsteps of all the good explorers by discovering the people, history and countryside of the land before it was 'discovered' by outside peoples, as well as telling the stories of the adventurers who travelled there for the first time.

Explorers have travelled all over the world and have been helped throughout the centuries by the inhabitants of the lands they visited. People have shown outsiders their homes, helped them carry their loads, paddled their canoes, showed them amazing animals and often housed, clothed, fed, rescued and cured them. This book tells you about these people as well as the explorers they helped or fought with.

Travellers have explored the world for many reasons. Early adventurers such as Marco Polo (1254–1324) and Ibn Battuta (1304–1364) journeyed with trading caravans. Christopher Columbus (1451–1506), Ferdinand Magellan (1480–1521), Captain James Cook (1728–1779) and John Franklin (1786–1847) were sent by governments to investigate the geography of the world. Other explorers were merchants, scientists, colonialists, artists, adventurers, naturalists or conquerors like Francisco Pizarro (1475–1541) who destroyed the Inca Empire that he discovered.

The Royal Geographical Society is proud to support the *Exploration Into* series of books. Ever since it was founded in 1830, the RGS has helped and inspired famous explorers such as Robert Scott (1868–1912) and Dr David Livingstone (1813–1873). Today, the RGS helps modern-day explorers climb the world's mountains, walk across its deserts, cycle through its continents, sail up its rivers, dive deep under the oceans and discover the scientific secrets of nature. We invite you to pick up *Exploration Into Japan* and start your own journey of discovery…

DR JOHN HEMMING,
Director and Secretary,
Royal Geographical Society, London

Contents

A sculpture of the priest Hoshi, whose face is splitting to reveal a deity.

1 Exploring Japan

Japan – A Nation Apart?

Japan stands apart, in the physical sense, as a group of islands. The country's borders are set by the sea. Japan's nearest neighbour, Korea, is over 190 kilometres away. The Japanese as a people also stand apart. Most countries in the world have minorities who differ from the majority population by reason of their race, religion or language. Japan has a population of over 123,000,000. Adding up all the minorities of every kind accounts for only about 2% of the population. Christians are the largest religious minority, and the largest ethnic minority are the 700,000 Koreans; but 90% of them were born in Japan and many have never been to Korea or learned to speak Korean. Only since the Second World War have the Japanese begun to travel overseas in large numbers or had the chance to meet foreigners, especially westerners, in Japan. For most of their history the Japanese have thought of themselves as a separate – and special – people.

A Language Apart

The Japanese language also helps to make the Japanese feel special because it is quite different from any other. **Pronunciation** is not difficult for speakers of European languages, but the grammar is extremely complicated. So is the system of writing. Before the Japanese made contact with China they had no way of writing their language. They took over the Chinese way of writing with characters (*kanji*) but also had to develop two additional syllabaries (*kana*), because Chinese and Japanese are very different languages, both in grammar and pronunciation. A syllabary is like an alphabet, but the symbols stand for syllables instead of separate single sounds. To be able to read a Japanese newspaper you need to know both kana and at least 3,000 characters. In this book Japanese names are given in the Japanese order – surname first.

The seasons in Japan are clearly marked and their changes have always been important subjects for Japanese poets and painters. The climate ranges from sub-tropical in Okinawa to sub-arctic in the Kuril Islands.

Japan is an **archipelago** of four main islands and over 4,000 small ones. About four-fifths of the country is mountainous, so most of the population is squeezed on to the coastal plains. Japan's rivers are mostly short and too shallow, swift or rock-filled to be of much use for transport. Coastal shipping was very important in linking major cities before railways were built in the 1870s.

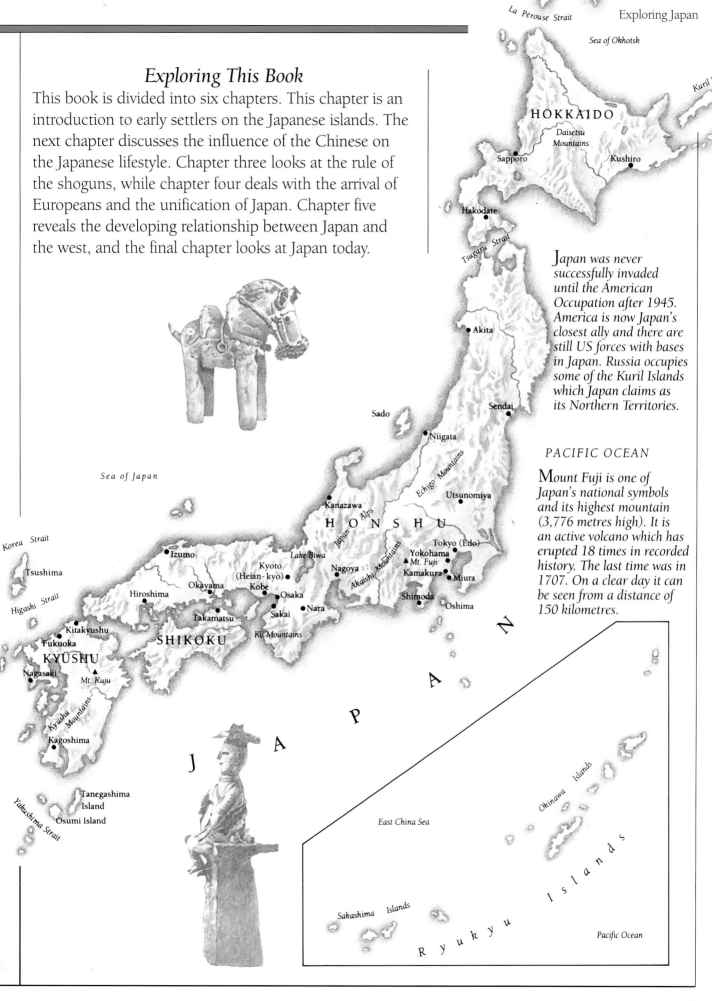

Exploring This Book

This book is divided into six chapters. This chapter is an introduction to early settlers on the Japanese islands. The next chapter discusses the influence of the Chinese on the Japanese lifestyle. Chapter three looks at the rule of the shoguns, while chapter four deals with the arrival of Europeans and the unification of Japan. Chapter five reveals the developing relationship between Japan and the west, and the final chapter looks at Japan today.

Japan was never successfully invaded until the American Occupation after 1945. America is now Japan's closest ally and there are still US forces with bases in Japan. Russia occupies some of the Kuril Islands which Japan claims as its Northern Territories.

PACIFIC OCEAN

Mount Fuji is one of Japan's national symbols and its highest mountain (3,776 metres high). It is an active volcano which has erupted 18 times in recorded history. The last time was in 1707. On a clear day it can be seen from a distance of 150 kilometres.

Map labels:

La Pérouse Strait
Sea of Okhotsk
Kuril Islands
HOKKAIDO
Daisetsu Mountains
Sapporo
Kushiro
Hakodate
Tsugaru Strait
Akita
Sendai
Sado
Niigata
Sea of Japan
Echigo Mountains
Utsunomiya
Kanazawa
Japan Alps
HONSHU
Izumo
Lake Biwa
Kyoto (Heian-kyo)
Nagoya
Akaishi Mountains
Tokyo (Edo)
Yokohama
Mt. Fuji
Kamakura
Miura
Korea Strait
Okayama
Kobe
Osaka
Shimoda
Tsushima
Hiroshima
Nara
Oshima
Higashi Strait
Takamatsu
Sakai
Kii Mountains
Kitakyushu
SHIKOKU
Fukuoka
KYUSHU
Nagasaki
Mt. Kuju
Kyushu Mountains
Kagoshima
J A P A N
Tanegashima Island
Osumi Island
Yakushima Strait
East China Sea
Okinawa Islands
Sakashima Islands
Ryukyu Islands
Pacific Ocean

Early Settlers

The Japanese islands have been inhabited for at least 30,000 years. Fossil remains of plants and animals show that Japan was once joined to the mainland of Asia. The earliest inhabitants probably **migrated** along land bridges which once joined southern Honshu to Korea and Hokkaido to Siberia. What is now the Sea of Japan would have been a huge lake. About 20,000 years ago great **glaciers** melted, raising the level of the sea and creating the straits which separate Japan's main islands from each other and the mainland.

From Hunters to Potters

The earliest inhabitants of Japan lived by hunting game and gathering wild plants. They used stone tools and weapons, but did not make pottery until around 10,000 BCE. The invention of pottery made it possible to improve ways of cooking and storing food. The pattern used to decorate pots at this time is known as Jomon, which means 'cord-marked'. The centuries up to 300 BCE are known as the Jomon period. Jomon people also made earthenware figures (*dogu*), which represented people or animals. Great piles of shells have been found at the sites of Jomon villages, showing that shellfish were an important part of their diet. Animal bones were used to make such things as needles and hairpins.

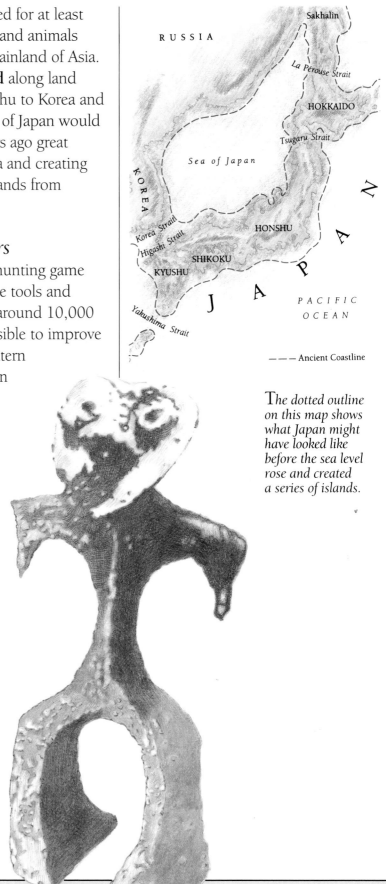

——— Ancient Coastline

The dotted outline on this map shows what Japan might have looked like before the sea level rose and created a series of islands.

This clay figure, called a dogu, *dates from the fourth century BCE, at the end of the Jomon period.*

The Ainu

One of the earliest groups of people to inhabit Japan were the Ainu. Most Japanese are descended from a mixture of **Mongol**, Malay and Polynesian peoples. The Ainu are quite clearly different and more like the peoples of Siberia. They are taller, more heavily built and have more facial and body hair than most Japanese. The Ainu language is quite different from Japanese and very few people speak it today. In the Ainu language the word 'ainu' simply means 'man'. In their religion the salmon, the owl, the killer whale and the bear were specially sacred. Bears were sacrificed to carry messages to their ancestors.

Nowadays about 25,000 Ainu still live in Hokkaido. They carve wooden bears to sell to Japanese tourists, who visit reconstructed Ainu villages.

Exploring the Ainu

One of the first people to study the Ainu way of life was an Englishman, John Batchelor (1854–1944). Although he had no proper schooling, he trained to become a **missionary** for the Church of England. In 1879 he came to Hokkaido to preach the gospel. To do this he had to learn the Ainu language. By 1889 he was able to publish an Ainu-English-Japanese Dictionary.

Batchelor built schools for the Ainu and gave them medical care. He lived among them for 60 years, until he was forced to leave when the Second World War broke out in 1939.

This early photo of an Ainu man was taken about 100 years ago. Notice his bushy beard. He wears boots and warm clothing to protect himself against the chilly climate of Hokkaido.

This detail from an eighteenth-century scroll shows an Ainu family. At this time only a few Japanese had any contact with the Ainu, who were regarded as primitive savages.

Rice and Emperors

The Japanese learnt the skill of rice-growing from the Chinese. These figures come from a Chinese painting. They are sorting the rice and transporting it.

This woman (below) is working in a flooded paddy-field, transplanting rice seedlings by hand. Transplanting was traditionally women's work.

Between 300 BCE and 300 CE the Japanese learned to grow rice, to work iron and bronze and to weave cloth. These advances had come from China, probably brought by migrant peoples moving into Japan from Korea or Okinawa. This period is called the Yayoi period, after a village called Yayoicho. When the village was **excavated**, **archaeologists** found a new kind of pottery, smooth and painted, quite different from the Jomon. They also found that bronze – a mixture of tin and copper – had been used to make mirrors, bells, swords and spears, and that iron had been used to make tools and farming implements.

Growing regular rice crops provided a more reliable food supply than hunting, so the population began to grow and people lived in larger villages. The leaders of the more powerful villages became chieftains, ruling over their neighbours. When they died, some were buried in mounds, which were separate from ordinary burial-grounds, to show that they were important.

The First Emperor

Every ancient people had a creation myth, explaining how the world began. The Japanese believed that it was created by gods who lived in heaven and that the sun goddess, Amaterasu, had given her grandson, Ninigi, a sword, a jewel and a mirror and sent him to rule over Japan. According to Japan's oldest history books, written in 712 CE and 720 CE, the first emperor, Jimmu, was Ninigi's grandson, who began his reign in 660 BCE. Japanese emperors are still given a sword, a jewel and a mirror when they come to the throne.

The key-hole shaped tomb said to have been built for the legendary emperor Nintoku around 400 CE. It is nearly 500 metres long and surrounded by three moats. Building it would have involved as much labour as building one of the Egyptian pyramids.

The Tomb Builders

Modern historians think that Japan's line of emperors can be traced back to about 400 CE, when a powerful family controlled an area of central Honshu called Yamato, which is the family name used by all emperors ever since. Between the fourth and seventh centuries the Japanese buried their rulers and nobles in huge tombs (*kofun*) guarded by clay figures called *haniwa* (see right).

This is a nineteenth-century coloured wood-block print showing the sun goddess, Amaterasu Omikami. Her name means 'great divinity illuminating heaven'.

Haniwa *clay figures, like this warrior, were placed around tombs as symbolic guards and servants.*

2 In the Shadow of China

Learning from China and Korea

A *Gagaku musician hitting a gong at the Shinto temple, Ise. Gagaku is an ancient form of court music in Japan.*

The Japanese began to have direct contact with China around 400 CE. China was much more powerful, wealthy and advanced than Japan. The Japanese were very impressed and eagerly learned how to write, how to make porcelain, silk, **lacquer** and paper and how to lay out (plan) cities. They also took over the Chinese calendar and the **Buddhist** religion (see right). For over 400 years Japan sent officials and scholars to China and in return welcomed many teachers, priests and craftsmen from there and Korea, who came to settle in Japan.

The Way of the Gods

The Japanese had their own religion, **Shinto**, which means 'the way of the gods'. It was based on the worship of nature and gods. Shinto had no great founder or prophet. It had no scriptures except myths that were eventually written down in the first Japanese books – the *Kojiki* and *Nihon shoki*. Shinto taught that every natural object, such as a lake or mountain, tree or rock, as well as any person either living or dead, had a spirit (*kami*) which ought to be respected. Many Shinto festivals and celebrations began as ways of asking the gods to protect the rice crop or thanking them for a good harvest.

The Great Buddha at Nara was built in the 8th century. It stands 16.2 metres high and is the world's largest statue of cast metal.

These are the Wedded Rocks at Futamigaura in Ise Bay. They are symbolic for Shinto followers, because people think that they sheltered the gods Izanagi and Izanami, the legendary creators of the islands of Japan.

Buddhism Comes to Japan

In 552 CE the king of Paekche in Korea sent some priests to the emperor of Japan with a statue of Buddha to explain the Buddhist religion. Buddha (**Enlightened** One) was the title given by his followers to an Indian teacher called Gautama. His teachings promised that if people lived a good, considerate and unselfish life they could escape being born over and over again, with all the pain, suffering and illness that went with human life. The Buddha died around 483 BCE, so Buddhism was already a thousand years old as a religion by the time it had spread through China and Korea to reach Japan.

Two Religions Side by Side

The Japanese were interested in Buddhism because it had a lot to teach about what happens to people when they die. Shinto was much more concerned about life in this world. So the two religions were thought to support each other. Japanese people came to believe that the Buddhist gods were Shinto spirits in another form. Nowadays most people still have a Shinto wedding and a Buddhist funeral.

An Age of Reform

Shotoku was a scholar who ruled as regent for Empress Suiko. His picture was used on Japanese banknotes until about five years ago.

Horyuji

The Horyuji Buddhist temple and monastery, near the ancient city of Nara, was first built in 607 by Prince Shotoku, a great patron of Buddhist learning. It burned down in 670, but was rebuilt immediately on an even larger scale and is now the oldest group of wooden buildings in the world. After his death, Shotoku was himself worshipped. Horyuji now has a great collection of 319 Buddhist art treasures and attracts thousands of visitors each year.

Horyuji's pagoda is the oldest in Japan. Pagodas were originally built over sacred relics associated with the Buddha. Horyuji became a famous centre for the study of Buddhism.

Prince Shotoku (574–622 CE) was interested in more than Buddhism. He also wanted to make the Japanese emperor as powerful in Japan as the Chinese emperor was in China. He introduced the Chinese idea of ruling through appointed officials rather than large landowners who could rebel against the emperor. Shotoku's plans were opposed by powerful courtiers who thought they would lose their positions. A determined effort to put the plans into practice was made in 646 in a series of **reforms** known as Taika ('great change'). All land was declared to belong to the emperor.

Peasants were to pay **taxes** in rice or cloth or by working on building projects or serving as soldiers. To help the emperor extend his rule over the whole country new roads were to be built and a postal service was established. A **census** of population was carried out in 670, so that the government could see how many taxpayers there were.

A Fixed Capital

Until the 7th century the Japanese usually moved their capital every time an emperor died, because they thought it would be unlucky to stay in the same place. But gradually the emperors came to accept the Chinese idea of a fixed capital. One reason for a fixed capital was that it was very inconvenient to keep moving all the government records. In 710 the Japanese laid out a capital at Nara. It had a grid plan, like the Chinese capital Chang'an (Xian), the largest city in the world at that time with a population of more than a million. By the middle of the century Nara had a population of 200,000.

This wooden sculpture in a temple at Nara shows a Buddhist saint meditating with his legs crossed. Buddhist monks shaved their heads as a sign of poverty and to show they had no interest in worldly matters.

First Geography Books

In 713 the Japanese government ordered the **governor** of each **province** to send in a detailed written report describing the land, animals, plants, products, place-names and legends of the area he was responsible for. The **survey** of land and resources was probably meant to help the government work out what taxes it could raise. The legends were written into the official history of the nation. Only five of the reports survive, more or less complete, although there were originally about 60.

An Emperors' Treasure House

The shosoin was built in 761 at Nara to store treasures belonging to the emperors. Made of cypress wood, it contains about 10,000 objects, including weapons, paintings, games, medicines, masks, pottery and musical instruments. Some of the treasures were made as far away as Persia.

Capital of Peace and Tranquillity

This map shows the spread of Buddhist monasteries during the seventh and eighth centuries. The names on the map represent provinces that were formed during the Nara period.

HOKKAIDO

Sea of Japan

HAGURO

HOKURIKUDO
TOZANDO
TOKAIDO

HONSHU

SANINDO KINAI
SANYODO   Heian-Kyo
Horyuji   Nara

NANKAIDO

SHIKOKU

SAIKAIDO
KYUSHU

Buddhism grew stronger throughout the Nara period thanks to the support of the emperor and his courtiers. Buddhist monasteries were built in each province and given lands to support them. Buddhist leaders became so powerful that they began to interfere in politics. In 784 Emperor Kammu (737–806) decided that the best way to escape from their influence was to move the capital again. In 794 the capital settled at Heian-kyo, which means 'capital of peace and tranquillity'. Later this city came to be known as Kyoto. In theory it remained the capital of Japan until 1868 because emperors continued to live there. The years from 794 to 1185 are known as the Heian period.

Court and Countryside

The emperor and his courtiers lived a life of luxury, cut off from ordinary people. They dressed exquisitely. Courtiers passed the time composing poems and writing them in beautiful **calligraphy**. A great deal of detail is known about life at the Heian court thanks to books written by courtiers, such as *The Tale of Genji*, a novel written by

The Tale of Genji

This book tells the life of Prince Genji, who is called the shining prince because he is brilliant at everything he does – poetry, painting, dancing, music and sport. Naturally he is also handsome and has beautiful manners. Although he has a successful career at court and is given many honours and gifts, he never really finds true happiness. Indirectly the story of Genji expresses the Buddhist idea that in the end human life is always sad. *The Tale of Genji* is a very long book, running to more than a thousand pages, with hundreds of different characters. It was written around 1000 CE and has been popular ever since.

Lady Murasaki Shikibu, and the diary kept by Sei Shonagon, another lady-in-waiting. Much less is known about the lives of the peasants who made up 90% of the population – except that they worked very hard and often suffered from plagues and attacks by bandits.

As the emperors preferred to pass their time studying or amusing themselves, the real power of appointing officials fell into the hands of court families, like the Fujiwara. They strengthened their hold on the emperors by marrying their daughters into the imperial family. Outside the capital itself power was in the hands of large landowners. In theory their land was a gift from the emperor and their titles meant that they were officials, appointed by the emperor. In practice both lands and titles were often passed on within families. They increased their land by draining marshes and cutting down forests. They had their own private armies to force the peasants to work for them. So the Fujiwara also had to use bands of warriors to enforce the commands they made in the name of the emperor.

This is a statue of the monk Kukai dressed as a pilgrim. Kukai established the famous pilgrimage route, visiting 88 temples, in his home island of Shikoku.

A Japanese Monk in China

In Japan the monk Kukai (774–835) is also known as Kobo Daishi (Great Teacher Kobo). In 804 he went with the official government mission to China to study Buddhism. But he was no ordinary student. He was an excellent poet, a brilliant calligrapher – and a fluent speaker of Chinese. When he went to Chang'an, the Chinese capital, the leading expert on Buddhism, Huiguo, welcomed him as a son. After two years Kukai returned to Japan and founded a monastery. In 823 the emperor invited him to become head of the most important monastery in Kyoto.

Japanese people believe that Kukai invented the *kana* system used in written Japanese (see page 4). He certainly compiled the oldest surviving Japanese dictionary. He also designed gardens and was a sculptor. Today the branch of Buddhism Kukai founded, Shingon (True Word), has 12,000,000 followers.

Priests of the Shingon sect, which has 12,000 temples. Shingon teaches that everything is made from six elements – earth, water, fire, wind, space and mind.

3 Shoguns and Samurai

The Rise of the Samurai

As the emperor's government in Kyoto grew weaker orders were still issued in his name, but they were often ignored outside the capital itself. The only taxes he could count on came from his own lands. The emperors, the Fujiwara family and other courtiers all came to rely on bands of **samurai** warriors to support them.

A portrait (bottom left) of Yoritomo, the head of the Minamoto clan, painted by the artist Fujiwara no Takanabu on a silk scroll 800 years ago.

For the samurai (below), the bow was as important a weapon as the sword. Their armour was so light and flexible that they could swim in it.

The Heike Wars

In 1156 a quarrel broke out at court about who should be the next emperor. The two fighting sides were the Taira family, who had gained power by acting as leaders of the emperor's army, and the Minamoto family, who were supported by the Fujiwara. For a while the Taira, under Kiyomori, made themselves supreme at court and persuaded the emperor to give them titles and grants of land. But in 1180 they tried to make one of their new-born children emperor. This was going too far and the Minamoto saw their chance to strike back, led by the cunning Yoritomo (1147–99). In 1181 Kiyomori died of fever. Without their leader the Taira were driven out of the capital by the Minamoto. The last great battle was fought at sea in 1185 at Dannoura, in the straits of Shimonoseki.

Tent Government

In 1192 Yoritomo persuaded the emperor to give him the title of **shogun**, which means 'great barbarian-conquering supreme general'. He established his permanent military headquarters at the coastal city of Kamakura because it was protected by mountains. For most of the next seven centuries the real power in Japan was in the hands of shoguns who gave orders in the name of the emperor. This system of ruling was known as the *bakufu* ('tent government') because generals gave orders from their tents when they were on campaign. Kamakura was now the real centre of government, although in theory Kyoto was still the capital and the emperor was still the ruler.

Minamoto rule did not last long. Yoritomo was succeeded by his two sons, but after the second one was **assassinated** in 1219, power passed to the family of Yoritomo's wife. These were the Hojo – who were related to the Taira!

The Samurai

Samurai means 'one who serves'. Bushi means 'fighting man'. Bushi is usually used to describe the warriors of the period up to the 1800s. They lived on their own lands when they were not actually fighting. Warriors of the later period generally lived in castle-towns and were paid in allowances of rice. They are referred to as samurai. These warriors were all expected to be fearless and loyal and to live plain, simple lives. They were expert horsemen and fought with swords, lances and bows. They were willing to kill themselves on the battlefield rather than face giving themselves up. The proper name for this is *seppuku*, but it has become known among westerners as *hara-kiri* (belly slitting).

A *photograph of Osaka castle (see also on page 24).*

Zen

A new kind of Buddhism became popular from the 12th century onwards – Zen. Traditional Buddhism had encouraged believers to study scriptures based on Buddha's sermons or to take part in ceremonies of chanting or dancing. Zen, which began in China, developed another practice – meditation. Meditation meant learning to sit entirely still and calm, to clear the mind of worry and fear. Zen made its followers try to look beyond the obvious, whether they were dealing with people or problems.

Zen monks meditating.

Art Among the Ashes

There was another side to Japan during these years of warfare and disorder. Towns and markets grew. Trade with China began again. Merchants formed **guilds** to organize business better. The fact that many people had time to go on pilgrimages suggests that some were more prosperous, as does the interest in new arts such as gardening and flower-arranging. Both these were strongly influenced by Zen (see panel), which encouraged people to see beauty in simple things.

Troubled Times

During the 13th century China was conquered by the Mongols. The Mongol emperor, **Kublai Khan**, decided he wanted to conquer Japan as well. In 1274 and 1281 he sent huge fleets to invade it. Each time the shogun gathered a great army to fight them off and spent a fortune on building defences along the coast. Each time the Mongol fleets were scattered by typhoons.

A New Bakufu

The expense of fighting off the Mongols led to heavy taxes. Heavy taxes led to rebellions. The Hojo family became more and more unpopular as government finances slid into chaos. The emperor Go-Daigo saw a chance to take power back into his own hands and in 1333 raised an army to challenge the Hojo. The Hojos sent a general called Ashikaga Takauji (1305–58) to put down the emperor's rising. Instead he joined the emperor's side. When they marched on the Hojos' headquarters, the Hojo all committed suicide.

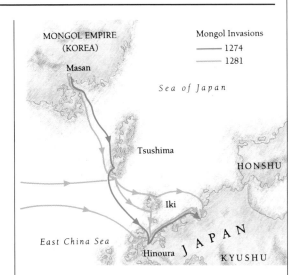

The Mongol invasions into Japan.

This print shows the Japanese monk Nichiren surrounded by Mongol warriors. Nichiren gained great influence when he correctly predicted that the Mongols would try to conquer Japan.

Go-Daigo soon made himself as unpopular as the Hojos. He gave all the most important jobs and estates to his courtiers and ignored the samurai generals who had put him back in power. In 1336 Ashikaga Takauji led a rebellion against Go-Daigo and forced him to flee to Yoshino, in the mountains south of Nara. From then until 1392 there were two imperial courts – a southern court at Yoshino and a northern one in Kyoto that gave the title of shogun to the Ashikaga family.

An Age of Chaos

In 1466 a quarrel broke out in the Ashikaga family over who was to be the next shogun. The outcome was the Onin war (1467–77), which reduced most of Kyoto to ashes. The Ashikaga became just one more warlord family among dozens of others, although they kept the title of shogun until 1588. For more than a century Japan was divided among ambitious soldiers. The most important warlords were called **daimyo**, which means 'great name'.

With no strong central government to suppress them the country was plagued by bandits and pirates. In the middle of all this chaos – and quite by accident – Japan suddenly made contact for the first time with Europeans.

Noh Drama

Noh is a kind of drama that began in fourth-century Kyoto. The actors were all men. They had gorgeous costumes and some wore masks. There was no scenery, except a painted background, but there were musicians who accompanied the actors as they chanted words and moved slowly. The stories for Noh plays often came from Buddhism. Troupes of Noh actors were employed by temples and shrines and performed at religious festivals. Noh is still performed by professional actors.

The Tea Ceremony

Tea was introduced to Japan from China in the Nara period and at first it was used as a medicine. The monk Eisai (1141–1215) is said to have brought tea seeds back with him in 1191 after visiting China. He and other monks believed that tea kept them alert while meditating. To fit the calm mood of meditation it became customary to prepare the tea in a slow, careful manner. Gradually the custom of preparing and drinking tea in quiet and tasteful surroundings spread to aristocrats and merchants. The greatest master of the tea ceremony (chanoyu) was a merchant, Sen-No Rikyu (1522–91). He believed that the most important part of the tea ceremony was not the implements people used, but the mood of relaxed appreciation they created. The tea ceremony remains extremely popular in Japan to this day.

4 The Coming of the Barbarians

Guns and Missionaries

The first Europeans to reach Japan were two Portuguese passengers aboard a Chinese **junk** which had to land at Tanegashima island, off Kyushu, to make repairs after a storm. This happened in 1543. The Portuguese at that time had a great fleet which was trying to control the highly profitable Asian spice trade. They had 'factories' (trading posts) from India to China. After their accidental contact with Japan, the Portuguese soon went back to find out what Japan had to offer.

The Japanese were certainly eager to trade for one thing – guns. They knew about gunpowder from the Chinese, who used it for making fireworks and signal-rockets. But before the arrival of the Portuguese, the Japanese had never seen a gun. Within six months of seeing one, Japanese **armourers** had learned how to make them.

The arrival of the Portuguese started a craze for imported novelties from Europe, such as clocks. Europeans also introduced products from other continents, such as carpets from the Middle East, tobacco from America and sweet potatoes from the Philippines.

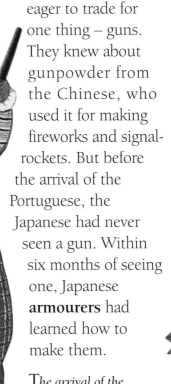

The warlord Oda Nobunaga (right) began the task of reuniting Japan. He is holding an iron fan for giving signals to troops on the battlefield. Oda was ambushed and killed during a tea ceremony.

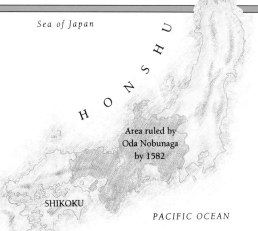

The warlord Oda Nobunaga managed to unite about a third of Japan.

A Revolution in Warfare

One of the first people to understand the importance of guns was the warlord Oda Nobunaga (1534–82). As early as 1549 he organized an infantry unit of 500 men, all armed with guns. His ambition was to put 'all the country under one sword' – his! Soon after guns came cannons, which again changed the nature of warfare.

In 1569 Oda captured the port of Sakai, an important centre for manufacturing guns and cannons. In 1575 he won a victory over his rivals at Nagashino, where he gathered 3,000 musketeers to wipe out a huge cavalry charge. By the time of his death Oda had managed to bring about a third of the country under his control.

Jesuit Missionaries

In 1549 **Jesuit** missionaries, led by St Francis Xavier, landed in Japan to **convert** the people to Christianity. There was no strong government to forbid them, but there was the problem of the Japanese language. The Jesuits found it so difficult that they said it must have been invented by the devil to stop them spreading the true religion. In 1603–1604 they finally printed a Portuguese-Japanese dictionary with 33,000 entries.

Southern Barbarians

The Japanese called the newcomers *namban*, which means 'southern barbarians', because they came to Japan from the south. All Japanese have black hair, so they were fascinated by the Portuguese with brown or blond hair. They were amazed by the dark skins of Indian and Indonesian sailors on Portuguese ships. You can see from the pictures they painted that they thought the strangers' baggy trousers were very odd and their pointed noses even odder!

Japan Unified

In 1582 Oda Nobunaga was assassinated by one of his own generals. He was soon revenged by another of his commanders, Toyotomi Hideyoshi (1536–98), an ugly little man whom Oda had nicknamed Monkey. But Toyotomi was a superb general. By 1587 he had added the southern island of Kyushu to Oda's conquests. By 1590 he controlled eastern Japan as well.

Toyotomi was determined to bring the civil wars to an end for good, so he ordered all peasants to give up their weapons and go back to farming. Samurai were ordered out of villages and told to live in castle-towns where they could be controlled by the daimyo who paid them. Toyotomi also ordered a detailed land survey and census so that he could set up an efficient tax system and work out how many samurai he could feed. His tax system lasted for the next 300 years. Peasants were guaranteed the right to work their land – at the price of being forbidden to leave it.

The sword is the soul of the samurai.

Conquering the World?

After he had united Japan, Toyotomi decided to attack Korea. In 1592 he sent 150,000 Japanese troops to Korea. The Koreans fought back, with Chinese support. The fighting was very savage and caused immense suffering. Gradually the Japanese were forced back. In 1598, as he was nearing death, Toyotomi ordered the Japanese to withdraw from Korea.

Toyotomi wanted to make sure that his lands went to his baby son, Hideyori. So he set up a **council** of five daimyo to make sure this happened. One of them was Tokugawa Ieyasu (1543–1616), his most trusted ally.

A Journey to Rome

By 1580 six daimyo had become Christians, possibly because they hoped to profit from trading with the Portuguese. Because they had converted, so had their samurai and servants, so that there were about 100,000 Japanese Christians. In 1582 four Japanese Christian boys were sent to Europe, where they were welcomed by Philip II of Spain and the Pope, Gregory XIII. They returned to Japan in 1590 and all four joined the Jesuit order.

This picture of Toyotomi makes him look calm and dignified. In fact he was a coarse and ill-mannered man, with a ferocious temper.

The invasion into Korea led by Toyotomi Hideyoshi.

Ieyasu was cool and calculating. The dynasty he founded ruled Japan for over 250 years.

Back to Front

The missionaries found many Japanese customs very strange and often just the opposite of the way things were in Europe. A Jesuit called Luis Frois made a list of them in the first history of Japan written by a westerner. He noticed that Japanese people preferred fish to meat and often ate it raw, whereas Europeans would only eat fish cooked. Japanese people **cremated** their dead, rather than burying them. Even the way they wrote their books was the opposite of the European way. The Japanese wrote from top to bottom rather than side to side and right to left, not left to right – which meant that, to Europeans, their books opened at the back, not the front!

The Last Bakufu

Ieyasu soon broke his promise to see that Hideyori inherited power. In 1600 he defeated Hideyori's supporters at the battle of Sekigahara, although Hideyori himself lived on. In 1603 Ieyasu asked the emperor to make him shogun. Ieyasu's family, the Tokugawa, were to rule as shoguns until 1868. Their bakufu headquarters at Edo became the real centre of power, just as Kamakura had (see page 17), although Kyoto was still, in theory, the capital. But unlike Kamakura, Edo grew to become Japan's biggest city. By 1750 it had a population of more than a million and was probably the largest city in the world.

In 1614 Ieyasu surrounded Hideyori's stronghold at Osaka castle and tricked him into filling in the moat. In 1615 the castle was taken and Hideyori killed himself. Ieyasu died the following year, having already passed on the title of shogun to his son.

The siege of Osaka castle caused huge damage, but the castle was rebuilt in 1620. Once Ieyasu had taken this last enemy stronghold, the power of the Tokugawa dynasty was finally secure. This painting is a detail from a folding screen.

This picture shows William Adams in 1600 talking to Ieyasu about a model of a European-style ship.

The Shogun's Englishman

William Adams (1564–1620) is the only foreigner ever to have been made a samurai. He came to Japan in 1600 as the pilot of a crippled Dutch ship which **beached** on Kyushu. The warlord Ieyasu questioned Adams, who told him a lot about European shipping and warfare. So Ieyasu ordered Adams to teach his men about gunnery and map-making. He also instructed him to build two European-style ships. For this reason the Japanese regard Adams as the founder of their navy.

Ieyasu refused to let Adams go back to England, but gave him an estate at Miura. Adams married the daughter of a Japanese official and had two children. He admired the Japanese and wrote that they were 'good of nature, courteous above measure and valiant in war'. The Japanese call him Miura Anjin – the pilot of Miura – and hold a ceremony in his honour every year at his grave.

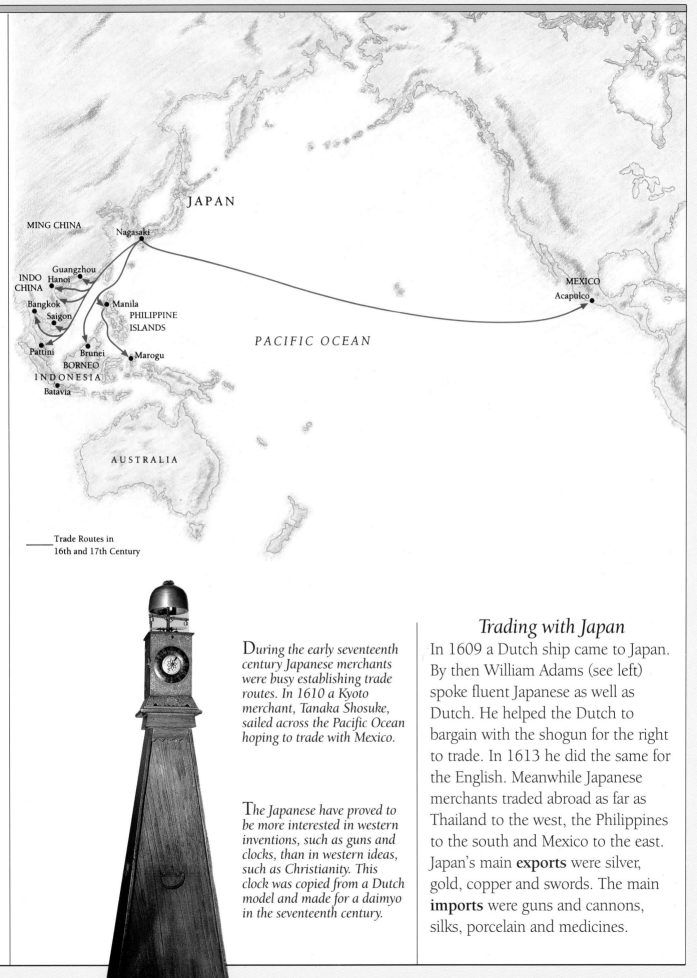

JAPAN

MING CHINA

Nagasaki

Guangzhou
INDO   Hanoi
CHINA

Bangkok   Manila
Saigon   PHILIPPINE
                    ISLANDS

Pattini   Brunei
BORNEO   Marogu
INDONESIA

Batavia

PACIFIC OCEAN

MEXICO
Acapulco

AUSTRALIA

Trade Routes in
16th and 17th Century

Trading with Japan

During the early seventeenth century Japanese merchants were busy establishing trade routes. In 1610 a Kyoto merchant, Tanaka Shosuke, sailed across the Pacific Ocean hoping to trade with Mexico.

The Japanese have proved to be more interested in western inventions, such as guns and clocks, than in western ideas, such as Christianity. This clock was copied from a Dutch model and made for a daimyo in the seventeenth century.

In 1609 a Dutch ship came to Japan. By then William Adams (see left) spoke fluent Japanese as well as Dutch. He helped the Dutch to bargain with the shogun for the right to trade. In 1613 he did the same for the English. Meanwhile Japanese merchants traded abroad as far as Thailand to the west, the Philippines to the south and Mexico to the east. Japan's main **exports** were silver, gold, copper and swords. The main **imports** were guns and cannons, silks, porcelain and medicines.

Closing the Country

The crucifixion of 26 martyrs at Nagasaki in 1597 marked the beginning of religious persecution.

So long as there was no strong government in Japan the Jesuits were free to preach. But as soon as Toyotomi Hideyoshi (see pages 22–23) had conquered Kyushu, where the Christians were most numerous, he began to **persecute** them. In 1597 he ordered 26 Christians, including nine European missionaries, to be crucified at Nagasaki. The Japanese government became increasingly worried that one of the Christian daimyo might try to start another war and bring in foreign troops.

But, Ieyasu thought that foreigners could be useful and kept them in their place by playing one off against another. His son, Hidetada, thought that Japan would be better off without them and cut down the trading rights of the English. Soon after Adams died the English closed their factory and left Japan.

Eyewitness for a Century

German-born Engelbert Kaempfer (1651–1716) qualified as a doctor before joining a Swedish **embassy** to Persia in 1683. From there he travelled through Thailand and Indonesia and reached Japan in 1690, where he worked as the doctor for the Dutch settlement at Dejima. In 1691 and 1692 Kaempfer joined the annual expedition which went to Edo to give presents to the shogun. This gave him a rare chance to see what Japan was like. He returned to Europe in 1693, smuggling out a collection of Japanese books and maps. Thirty-five years later he published a two-volume *History of Japan* (1727–28) based on his collection of Japanese materials and his experiences. It appeared in Dutch, French and German editions and remained the standard European work on Japan for over a century.

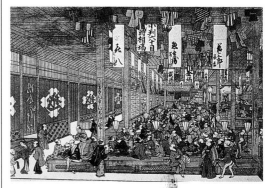

A 'hundred things shop' (department store) in seventeenth-century Edo.

When a new shogun, Iemitsu, came to power in 1623, he celebrated by having 50 Christians killed. Between 1633 and 1639 his government issued a series of laws. These forbade the Japanese to go abroad or, if they were abroad, forbade them to return on pain of death. They forbade the building of ocean-going ships, Christianity and limited foreign trade to the Dutch and Chinese.

The Dutch at Dejima

In 1641 the Dutch were ordered to move their trading-post to Dejima, an artificial island in Nagasaki harbour, paid for by 25 wealthy Japanese merchants who benefited from overseas trade. This tiny patch of land was to be the only place foreigners were allowed to live in Japan until 1854. No other Europeans were allowed to trade with Japan at all. As far as the Japanese were concerned foreign trade was a luxury, not a necessity.

A Dutch sailing ship with flags flying.

Japanese often like to use short poems as pieces of calligraphy and accompany them with sketches. The aim of this is to use a few words and brushstrokes to suggest much more than is said or shown.

A Poet on the Move

Matsuo Basho (1644–94) is known to all Japanese as the great master of haiku, a form of short poem which has three lines of five, seven and five syllables. Haiku are like snapshots which record a single moment or feeling, rather than tell a story.

Basho became a popular teacher of haiku in Edo and lived well. But success made him feel that he was becoming lazy. For the last ten years of his life he took to travelling in the hope that seeing nature first-hand would help him write better poetry. Basho wrote accounts of his travels which were a mixture of diary, poems and descriptions of places he had seen.

Basho's greatest journey took him to the remotest parts of Honshu, over the mountains and along the Japan Sea coast, covering 2,400 kilometres in 156 days. His account of this, *The Narrow Road to the Deep North,* was published in the year of his death. It shows how much the poet was moved by the beauty of Japan's landscape and its history.

Know Your Place!

The ideas of Confucius governed Japanese society during the period of Tokugawa rule. All educated samurai read his writings.

The main aim of the Tokugawa government (1603–1868) was peace. They controlled about a quarter of all the land and around their own holdings they created barrier lands held by their most trusted followers (*fudai*), daimyo who had fought on their side at Sekigahara (see page 24). Their former enemies were treated as 'outer lords' (*tozama*) and left to rule estates on the fringes of the country. Spies and informers were used to guard against unauthorized **fortifications** or marriage alliances between powerful families.

A Confucian Society

The Tokugawa government supported the ideas of the ancient Chinese scholar **Confucius** (551–479 BCE), who thought disorder was the greatest evil and praised loyalty and obedience. Samurai were at the top of society because they ruled. Next came farmers, who produced food, then craftsmen, who made things. Merchants came below craftsmen, because they didn't make anything. Scholars, doctors and priests were on the same level as samurai, because they usually came from samurai families and were educated. Women were always supposed to obey men.

Strengths and Weaknesses

That was the theory. In practice peace enabled trade to prosper and many merchants became very wealthy. As samurai borrowed money from them, the merchants used their debts to gain power over them. Peasants didn't always put up with their hard life and there were more than 2,000 revolts during Tokugawa times. One reason for this was that without foreign trade Japan was running out of food. A series of bad harvests in the 1780s and 1830s led to famines and epidemics.

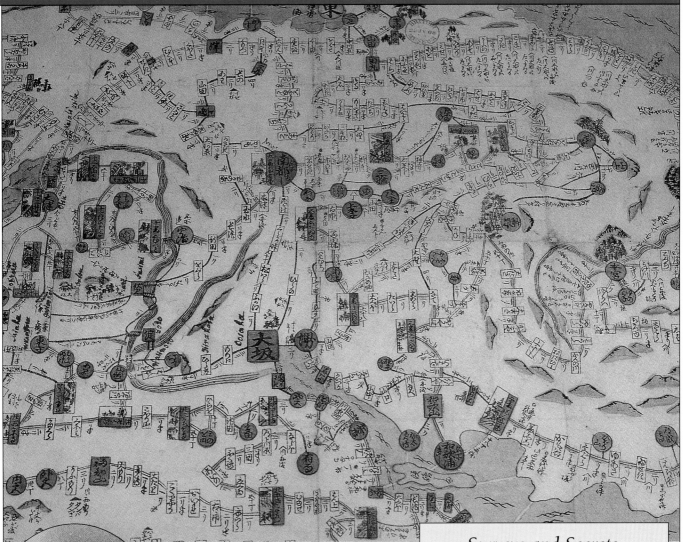

This Japanese map dates from around 1820.

The Founding Father

The founding father of the study of Japan was the German Philipp Franz von Siebold (1796–1866). Like Kaempfer he was employed by the Dutch East India Company as a doctor for the trading post at Dejima, where he arrived in 1823. A year later he set up a college where he taught western medicine to the Japanese in return for their reports on Japan and its people. One of von Siebold's pupils, Ito Gemboku (1800–1871), went on to pioneer **vaccination** against smallpox in Japan. The centre he set up for this became Tokyo University's School of Medicine.

Philipp von Siebold

Ito Gemboku

Surveys and Secrets

Ino Tadataka (1745–1818) was the first person to produce a complete survey of Japan using western, scientific methods – and he didn't start it until he was nearly 50. Ino studied with the shogun's official astronomer, Takahashi Yoshitoki, who had some Dutch books about astronomy and surveying.

By the time he was 70 Ino had spent 3,737 days on the road, taking measurements and had walked 43,700 kilometres. Ino died in 1818, but his death was kept secret by his devoted **disciples** until his great work was finished and published in 1821 by Takahashi Kageyasu, who had followed his father as official astronomer. Takahashi also added information about the northern islands of Hokkaido and Sakhalin. Ino's maps were still in use 100 years after his death.

5 Opening Up

Intrusion and Revolution

In 1846 the American government decided that it was time Japan opened up to foreigners. In July 1853 four American warships anchored off Edo. Their commander, Commodore Matthew Perry, delivered a message asking for trading rights and promising to return the following year for an answer. In February 1854 he came back with eight ships. They brought many gifts, including a miniature railway with 100 metres of track. They also gave demonstrations of military **drill**. The message was fairly clear. Agree – or else!

The shogun's government agreed to sign a **treaty** which allowed American ships to visit the ports of Shimoda and Hakodate to buy supplies and offer fair treatment to shipwrecked sailors. The treaty also allowed the Americans to have a **consul** living at Shimoda to look after American interests. By 1856 Britain, France, Russia and the Netherlands all had similar treaties. In 1858 the shogun's government agreed to open more ports and gave the foreigners further rights. Many samurai found these 'unequal treaties' bitterly humiliating.

These three prints show London, painted by a Japanese artist who had never seen it. Notice the warships and soldiers, showing Britain as a war-like country.

A contemporary Japanese print showing one of Commodore Perry's ships in Edo bay.

The Meiji Restoration

Japan was deeply divided by the coming of the westerners. Many samurai wanted to drive them back into the sea.

Japan's crisis was settled by a brief civil war in 1867–68. Led by the Choshu and Satsuma clans, an army of samurai overthrew the Tokugawa. To make it clear that this was in the best interests of Japan, they claimed they were restoring power to where it rightly belonged – with the emperor. In Japan emperors choose a name for their reign (*nengo*), and the teenage emperor decided to call his reign Meiji, which means 'Enlightened Rule'. The emperor moved from Kyoto to Edo – which then became Tokyo, which means 'Eastern Capital'.

The Iwakura Mission

In 1871 a high-level mission of 50 **diplomats**, experts and interpreters was sent to the west to see whether the 'unequal treaties' signed by the shogun's government

could be revised. Attempts to revise the treaties were dropped after the USA made it clear that they would not consider it. So the mission concentrated on visiting factories, schools, hospitals and other institutions to see how they worked and how Japan might benefit from western technology and institutions. They returned home determined to enrich the country and strengthen the army. By then Japan's modernization was well under way.

Even before the return of the Iwakura mission great changes were taking place. After its return they happened even faster. In 1870 Tokyo and the new port of Yokohama were linked by telegraph, and a railway between the two was opened in 1872. In 1876 samurai were forbidden to wear swords. The first Japanese newspaper was published in 1871. In 1872 the first modern census showed that Japan had a population of 33,110,825. The western calendar was adopted in 1873, the same year in which the emperor and empress started to wear western-style dress, rather than traditional Japanese costumes.

Enough!

For many Japanese these changes were going too far, too fast. In 1874 there was a rebellion by discontented samurai. In 1876 there were three more rebellions. The last and greatest was led by a hero of the civil war that had put the modernizing government in power – Saigo Takamori (1827–77). His army of 40,000 samurai was beaten by the new army of peasant **conscripts** in western-style uniforms. He committed suicide on the battlefield.

Saigo's defeat did not mean the end of the samurai, although they did lose their privileges. Only a few could become officers in the new army. Others became policemen, postmasters or railway officials. Thousands became teachers. They taught their pupils to behave as they had been taught – to be brave, loyal and hard-working.

Saigo Takamori – a samurai rebel against too much change.

Civilization and Enlightenment

The craze for western things reached its height in the 1880s. Japan's rulers seemed convinced that western countries were the source of every kind of 'civilization and enlightenment'. In 1883 the government opened the Rokumeikan (Pavilion of the Deer's Cry), a western-style building where Japanese – in western dress – could meet foreigners to dance, listen to concerts, play cards and raise money for charities. Japanese writers began to write poems and novels in the western style. In 1889 the emperor granted a **constitution** with an elected parliament, called the National Diet.

Japan's Leading Westernizer

Fukuzawa Yukichi (1835–1901) learned Dutch when he was 20. When he discovered that Holland was then, politically, a much less important country than Britain or America, he immediately began to learn English. In 1860 he went with the first Japanese mission to America and in 1862 travelled with the first mission to Europe. In 1867 he began to publish a ten-volume series called *Conditions in the West*. The first volume sold 150,000 copies. But Fukuzawa was not popular with everyone. For over ten years he was unable to go out at night for fear of being murdered by samurai who opposed westernization.

Young Fukuzawa, wearing the sword of the samurai.

Japan's National Diet and constitution were based on that of Germany – another country led by an emperor and determined to become a great modern power.

This photo was taken in the nineteenth century and shows Japanese country life as it was then. Little had changed for many years, proving that the majority of change was happening in the cities and among court and government officials.

Fukuzawa continued to write and spread his ideas by founding a newspaper and a leading university, Keio. He was in favour of women's rights and believed that one of the things the new Japan needed most was people who were completely free and unafraid to speak out.

Keep Japan Japanese!

The geographer Shiga Shigetaka (1863–1927) grew up at the height of the craze for western things. In 1886 he travelled through the South Pacific. Everywhere he saw that the local people were doing all the hard work while the westerners grew rich. When he came home, he wrote *Conditions in the South Seas* to warn Japanese people against the danger of falling under western control.

In 1888 Shiga helped to found the Society for Political Education to spread this message, to oppose the 'unequal treaties' and to campaign against pollution and in favour of Japan acquiring her own colonies overseas. He became a lecturer in geography at Waseda University. In 1894 he published a book about Japan's landscape, which created much public interest in mountaineering and led to his appointment as head of the Forestry Bureau at the Ministry of Agriculture. Britain honoured him by making him an Honorary Fellow of the Royal Geographical Society.

Change and Old Ways

The 1880s were the high point of the craze for change. However, the different attitudes that Japanese had towards change can be seen in the contrasting careers of Ito Hirobumi (1841–1909) and Itagaki Taisuke (1837–1919). Both men took part in the wars that overthrew the Tokugawa bakufu and served as ministers in the new government that was modernizing Japan. Itagaki took a leading part in calling for a parliament and founded Japan's first modern political party. He spent much of his later career in opposition,

The *Japanese parliament was formed by those who overthrew the Tokugawa bakufu.*

criticizing the government. Ito was the man who wrote the constitution that gave Japan a parliament. He served four times as prime minister, but was suspicious of party politics and believed that political leaders should think of themselves as servants of the emperor.

Live Machines

The rush to modernize meant that Japan had to import foreign experts as teachers, technicians, and advisers. They were addressed as 'Honorable Foreign Expert', but behind their backs they were sometimes referred to as 'live machines'. The Japanese employed more than 4,000 of them, about half of them British. The Japanese chose their experts very carefully. The British were selected for their knowledge of navigation, shipbuilding, railways, lighthouses, steel-making and drains. French and Germans were employed as soldiers, doctors and experts on local government. Americans were hired as experts on education and agriculture. The Japanese were determined to learn from foreigners, not to rely on them.

Ito Hirobumi *believed that political leaders should be loyal to the emperor.*

America's 'Japan Man'

W.E.Griffis (1843–1928) was in Japan for less than four years, but his 18 books and hundreds of magazine articles about the country made him recognized as America's leading expert. He saw at first hand how quickly the country had changed from disorder and poverty to a wealthy industrialized nation. He also realized that 'the Japanese simply want helpers and advisers. They propose to keep the "bossing"… and all the power in their own hands.' Within two years of getting home he published *The Mikado's Empire*, which had been reprinted 12 times by 1913. The Japanese government twice honoured him with the Order of the Rising Sun, an official decoration to recognize his services to Japan.

*J*apan on the move! Wheeled vehicles, railways and ocean-going ships were all new to Japan. They speeded up communications and put Japan in touch with the wider world.

Things Japanese

The British equivalent of Griffis was Basil Hall Chamberlain (1850–1935), whose humorous dictionary *Things Japanese* (1890) went through six editions. By the time he left Japan in 1911 he had risen from instructor in English at the navy school to become the first Professor of Japanese at Tokyo University, where he pioneered the study of early Japanese history, poetry and language.

Rescuing the Past

What Chamberlain did for literature, two Americans did for archaeology and art. Edward S. Morse (1838–1925) came to Japan in 1877 to teach zoology, but as soon as he arrived he also conducted Japan's first archaeological dig at Omori. Before he left in 1880 he helped to found Japan's first modern museum. In 1886 he published *Japanese Homes and their Surroundings*, which introduced western readers to Japanese architecture.

Ernest Fenellosa (1853–1908) was invited to Japan to teach **economics**, but he soon became a passionate defender of traditional Japanese art. Fenellosa used his position at the Ministry of Education to reintroduce Japanese-style art lessons in school and to persuade the government to control the export of works of art. He also helped to found the college that became the Tokyo University of Fine Arts and Music and wrote books about Japanese wood-block prints and traditional Noh drama (see page 18).

Globe Trotters

*Sir Rutherford
Alcock*

Britain's first diplomat in Japan was Sir Rutherford Alcock (1809–97). In 1863 Alcock published an account of his time in Japan, *The Capital of the Tycoon*. Like Frois (see page 23), he portrayed it as a topsy-turvy land in which everything seemed to be the wrong way round. 'There old men fly kites while the children look on; the carpenter uses his plane by drawing it to him and their tailors stitch from them; they mount their horses from the off-side – the horses stand in the stables with their heads where we place their tails … ladies black their teeth instead of keeping them white …' And as for men and women mixing together naked in the public bath-houses … words failed him. What serious traveller could resist such a fascinating country?

Gilbert and Sullivan's comic opera The Mikado *took advantage of Britain's 1880s craze for Japanese things. The authentic costumes were supplied by Libertys of Regent Street, London, who specialized in importing real Japanese silks and fans.*

Unbeaten Tracks in Japan

Isabella Bird (1831–1904) certainly couldn't resist the challenge of Japan and found her 2,300 kilometres horse-back trek through northern Honshu and Hokkaido thoroughly worth the effort: 'Japan offers as much novelty perhaps as an excursion to another planet.' But she didn't always like or approve of what she saw: 'The Japanese are the most irreligious people that I have ever seen – their pilgrimages are picnics, and their religious festivals fairs.'

Isabella Bird

Dolls' Houses

In 1889 the writer Rudyard Kipling stopped off in Japan on his way from India to England. The contrast with India was striking: 'It is strange to be in a clean land and stranger to walk among dolls' houses. It would pay us to … take away any fear of invasion … and pay the country as much as ever it chose, on condition that it simply sat still and went on making beautiful things.'

Japonisme

Japan's biggest impact on westerners was in the field of art. European artists were fascinated by the brightly-coloured wood-block prints (*ukiyo-e*) produced by artists such as Hokusai (1760–1849) and Hiroshige (1797–1858). They first came to Europe as packaging wrapped round porcelain bowls and vases. More than a hundred were exhibited at the 1867 Paris *Exposition Universelle*. French artists, such as Claude Monet and Edgar Degas, were keen collectors. The French art critic Burty called their craze Japonisme. In Britain the fashion was spread by the American artist James Whistler. His paintings not only show wood-block prints, but also Japanese vases and flower arrangements, and models wearing **kimono** and holding Japanese fans.

This painting of dancers by Edgar Degas was influenced by Japanese art.

First Impressions

Lafcadio Hearn (1850–1904) was an Irish-Greek who lived in America and the West Indies before landing in Japan in 1890. He was absolutely enchanted and wrote an excited essay 'My First Day in the Orient':

'… everything Japanese is delicate, exquisite, admirable – even a pair of common wooden chopsticks in a paper bag with a little drawing on it. The bank bills, the commonest copper coins are things of beauty. Even the piece of plaited coloured string used by the shopkeeper in tying up your last purchase is a pretty curiosity.' Hearn never left Japan. He married a Japanese and became a Japanese citizen in 1896, taking the name Koizumi Yakumo. He became an expert on Japanese legends and customs.

Photographing Japan

If there was ever a really serious visitor it was Herbert G. Ponting, a Fellow of the Royal Geographical Society, who spent three years in Japan so that he could 'photograph the country to my heart's content'. The result was a book of nearly 400 pages, *In Lotus Land* (1909). Photography wasn't always easy. In Kyoto he was moved on by the police when he tried to take a picture of a holy procession. At Osaka Castle he was arrested by the army, who thought he was a Russian spy. The first time he tried to take views of the inside of a volcanic crater, he was dismayed to find that the sulphurous fumes ruined his photographic plates.

Herbert Ponting *trying to photograph a volcano. Many aspects of 'old Japan' were recorded by keen western photographers just before they disappeared forever.*

Alliance and Defiance

The late 19th and early 20th centuries were dominated by war with other countries. In the 1880s Japanese generals became very concerned about Korea, a weak and backward kingdom that was also the nearest part of Asia to Japan. Both China and Japan interfered in Korean politics. In 1894 they went to war over who was to control it. Japanese forces, although outnumbered, won easily. The island of Formosa (Taiwan) was handed over and became a Japanese colony.

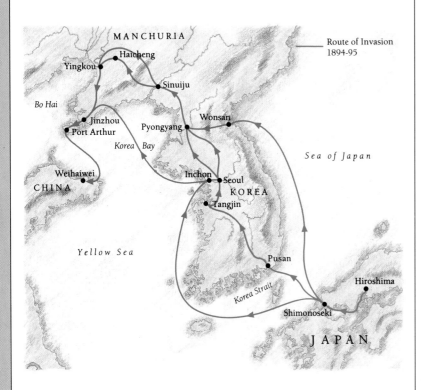

Japan fought twice to gain control of Korea, which it called 'a dagger point at the heart of Japan' (left).

A popular print of the naval battle in the Sea of Japan in 1905 where Admiral Togo defeated the Russians (above).

War with Russia

In 1904–1905 Japan fought Russia over Korea and won again, though it was a much harder fight. Japan gained the southern half of Sakhalin (see page 29). In 1910 Korea became a Japanese colony. The Koreans resisted but were crushed. In Taiwan, by contrast, Japan helped improve conditions by building roads, schools and hospitals and encouraging better farming methods.

By 1911 all the western powers had agreed to abolish the 'unequal treaties' signed back in the 1850s. Many Japanese drew the conclusion that aggression was the best way for a nation to be respected.

A postcard drawn in 1905 showing the Japanese supremacy over the Russians.

The Road to War

During the First World War Japan fought on the Allied side. In 1919 at the Paris Peace Conference Japan was treated as one of five great powers. The conference formed a new League of Nations, to settle international disputes. However, the collapse of world trade between 1929 and 1931 led to political crises in every major country. In Japan there was mass unemployment. Junior officers in the army demanded that Japan enlarge her Asian empire by force as a way of solving the nation's problems. Politicians who opposed this were murdered.

In 1931 Japanese forces in Asia invaded the Chinese province of Manchuria. The government in Tokyo was too weak to stop them. In 1932 a **puppet-state** of Manchukuo was set up, with real power in Japanese hands.

A Japanese wood-block print shows Japanese Red Cross nurses helping the wounded in the Sino-Japanese war.

In 1923 an earthquake hit Tokyo, which added to Japan's troubles.

Japan at War

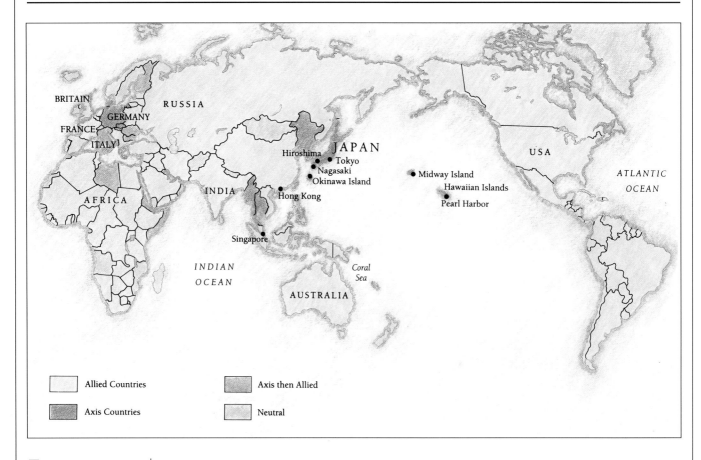

Allied Countries

Axis Countries

Axis then Allied

Neutral

The map above shows the various alliances of countries during the Second World War.

Below is a print of the Japanese surprise air attack on Pearl Harbor, Hawaii on 7 December 1941.

When the League of Nations condemned the invasion of China, Japan left the League and in 1936 allied itself with the other war-like powers, Germany and Italy.

In 1937 an all-out invasion of China was launched. The United States tried to force Japan to pull back by cutting off supplies of steel and then oil. Believing that war with the United States was unavoidable Japan launched a surprise attack on the US naval base at Pearl Harbor, Hawaii, on 7 December 1941.

Victory and Defeat

For six months after Pearl Harbor the Japanese forces seemed unstoppable, taking Hong Kong and then, in February 1942, Singapore, the main British base in eastern Asia. Soon they threatened the borders of India. But the great naval battles of the Coral Sea and Midway Island in the summer of 1942 destroyed the Japanese navy's striking power. The Allies were at last free to strike back, re-taking Pacific islands until they could establish bases from which Japan could be attacked and bombed.

A three-day raid on Tokyo in March 1945 killed more than 100,000 people. The Japanese prepared to resist the invasion of their homeland. Young pilots volunteered for suicide missions against Allied shipping. Two thousand planes flew in these attacks, sinking 34 ships and damaging 288 more. In defending the island of Okinawa the Japanese lost 100,000 soldiers and 150,000 civilians, many in mass-suicides of schoolchildren and nurses.

Japan's eventual surrender was forced by the dropping of **atomic bombs** on Hiroshima and Nagasaki in August 1945 and Russia's declaration of war, followed by occupation of the Kuril Islands

The scene after an atomic bomb at Hiroshima. Two atomic bombs were dropped, one here and the other at Nagasaki. They were so powerful that they created huge fireballs which destroyed everything except concrete buildings.

(see page 4). Faced with the possibility of being divided between occupying powers, and having the imperial court abolished, Japan finally laid down its arms and waited for the unknown.

After Japan's surrender in 1945, the Allied forces moved into Japan and took control of the government.

6 The New Japan

Modernization

During the Allied **Occupation** of 1945–52 Japan adopted a new democratic constitution which gave equal rights to all citizens, including women. Reforms were passed that improved education and gave land to farmers. As soon as the Occupation ended, Japan signed an alliance with her former enemy, the USA, who now became her biggest trading partner.

This officially sponsored photograph represented an ideal view of the new, post-war Japan – the perfect timing of the super-express Bullet train and the timeless perfection of Mount Fuji. This picture was published around the world in books and posters.

Recovery

By 1955 the output of Japanese industry had risen to the levels of 1936. Rapid economic growth soon made Japan a world leader in ship-building, steel, cameras and electrical goods. In 1958 Japan launched the world's largest oil-tanker. By 1964 Japan was ready to go on show to the world as the host of a highly-successful Olympic games. The 200 km/h bullet train service which began that year became a symbol of Japan's efficiency and advanced technology. The first industrial robot came into use in 1970. Less welcome was the pollution which was a damaging side-effect of industrial expansion.

Oil Shocks

The quadrupling of oil prices in 1973 hit Japan hard because almost all of its energy was imported. In 1979 there was a second oil shock. Industry responded by cutting back on manufacturing, which needed large amounts of oil – such as steel and chemicals – and expanding those which depended instead on skilled labour, such as machinery, electronics and computers. These high-tech industries also had the added advantage of causing far less pollution than oil-based industries.

The opening ceremony of the 1964 Olympic Games, hosted in Tokyo. The 19-year-old torch-bearer was born in Hiroshima on the day the atomic bomb was dropped.

Internationalization

By the 1970s Japanese companies were beginning to set up in business abroad, partly to be nearer their markets, partly to take advantage of lower prices for land, labour and materials. Northern Europe, the United States and South-East Asia were especially favoured areas for Japanese **investment**. Japan also became the world's largest giver of foreign aid by 1988.

In 1992 a change in the law allowed 2,000 Japanese troops to operate overseas and take part in United Nations (UN) peace-keeping operations in Cambodia, mostly providing technical services as engineers. This was a small but important step towards playing a much bigger part in tackling international problems.

Japan Today

Mass-production of electrical goods made Japan's economy strong in the 1960s. Other important products were steel, ships and cameras. Today Japan is a leading producer of computers and industrial robots.

Kendo – the way of the sword. Japanese fencing, like judo, ikebana, origami and karaoke, has won enthusiastic fans around the world, as have the growing of miniature trees (bonsai) and the writing of haiku poems.

By the mid-1980s Japan had proved itself as a highly efficient modern nation accounting for a tenth of the world's entire annual output. Its average annual income per head was higher than that of the USA. Japanese tourists became an important source of income for neighbouring Asian countries, Australia, Hawaii and Europe. Japanese businesses relocated factories overseas, not only to take advantage of lower labour costs in some Asian countries, but also to get closer to their markets in North America and Western Europe. Today, despite having some of the most advanced factories in the world, Japan's traditional crafts are still produced in small workshops and sold in tiny shops in the country's modern high-rise cities.

Recently Japan's prosperity was challenged by increased competition from such neighbours as South Korea, Singapore and Malaysia. The necessity of supporting an ageing population has also increased the pressure on the economy.

Exploring Japanese Culture

Japan's rising international profile is reflected in growing foreign interest in its culture. Judo and kendo has gained Olympic status. Carp-breeding, flower-arranging, origami (paper-folding), composing haiku poems and growing bonsai

The ultra-modern high-tech architecture of industrialized Japan.

A display of kumade on sale at a Shinto temple. They are good luck charms.

(miniature trees) all have keen followings outside Japan. Karaoke singing is popular with Western adults, while younger fans eagerly play Japanese computer games or collect Pokemon cards.

Japan's International Role

The admiration of the outside world has given many Japanese renewed pride in their achievements. However, people realised there was a price to pay for a modern, industrial way of life with congested cities, pollution and environmental damage. In 1997 Japan took an important international initiative in hosting a world conference on climate change in Kyoto. Many leading nations pledged to help slow down global warming.

Japan also held the very successful 1998 Winter Olympics and in 2002 co-hosted the soccer World Cup.

Politics

In 1993 the Liberal Democrats Party, who had governed Japan since 1955, lost power after a series of scandals. Short-lived governments have since then promised political reform but it is yet to be achieved.

Despite these problems, Japan's successful blend of the traditional and the modern will help the country face up to the challenges of the 21st century.

Japan	Europe	Other
c.8000 BCE First pottery made in Japan.	**c.6500** BCE Farming begins in Greece and spreads to other areas of Europe.	**c.9000** BCE Hunters spread throughout North and South America.
600 BCE Traditional date of first emperor, Jimmu.	**c.1600** BCE Mycenean civilization begins in Greece.	**c.650** BCE Iron is being used in China.
c.400 CE Emergence of Yamato rule	**452** CE Atilla the Hun enters Italy.	**30** CE Death of Jesus Christ. Spread of Christianity begins.
c.550 Introduction of Buddhism.	**c.542** Bubonic plague spreads through Europe.	**622** Muhammad founds the religion of Islam in Arabia.
607 First official mission to China.	**597** St Augustine lands in England with 30 missionaries.	**935** The text of the Quran finished.
741 Provinces ordered to build Buddhist monasteries.	**757** Offa becomes king of Mercia in England.	**c.1000** The Vikings colonize Greenland and travel to America.
1192 Shogun rule established.	**1066** The Normans conquer England.	**1352** Ibn Battuta travels to Africa.
1467 Beginning of civil wars.	**1492** The first globe is made in Germany by Martin Beheim.	**1368** Ming Dynasty in China.
1543 First Europeans reach Japan.	**1532** John Calvin starts the Protestant movement in France.	**1492** Christopher Columbus reaches the Americas.
1590 Unification of Japan complete.	**1618** The Thirty Years War of religion starts.	**1607** The first English settlement is founded in America (Virginia).
1639 Japan closed to foreign contacts.	**1667** The French begin to expand under Louis XIV.	**1644** Manchu Dynasty in China.
1853 Commodore Perry's ships open up Japan.	**1707** England and Scotland unite.	**1680** Rozvi Empire in Zimbabwe.
1868 The Meiji restoration.	**1789** The French Revolution begins.	**1775** The American Revolution begins.
1889 New constitution adopted.	**1833** The slave trade is abolished in Britain.	**1789** George Washington becomes the first President of the United States.
1894-95 War against China.	**1884-85** The African conference is held in Berlin (Germany).	**c.1700s** The European exploration of Africa begins.
1904-5 War against Russia.	**1901** Queen Victoria dies.	**1861** The American Civil War begins.
1910 Korea becomes a colony.	**1914-18** The First World War.	**1917** The USA enters The First World War.
1941 Attack on Pearl Harbour.	**1939-45** The Second World War.	**1941** The USA enters The Second World War.
1972 Okinawa reverts to Japan.	**1961** The Berlin Wall is built in Germany.	**1961** John F. Kennedy becomes President of the USA.
1973 and **1979** Oil shocks.	**1972** The European Community gains more members.	**1963** John F. Kennedy is assassinated.
1986 Twelfth Summit Conference held in Tokyo.	**1985** Mikhail Gorbachev becomes the leader of the Soviet Union.	**1965-73** The United States is involved in the Vietnam War.
1989 Death of Emperor Hirohito (Showa).	**1989** Berlin Wall is destroyed. **1990** East and West Germany reunited.	**1989** Tianamen Square massacre in China. **1990** Nelson Mandela is released.
1993 Marriage of Crown Prince Naruhito to a commoner, Miss Owada Masako.	**1991-4** Breakup of Yugoslavia.	**1991** Gulf War to liberate Kuwait from Iraqi invasion.
1995 Kobe earthquake kills 5,000. **1997** Japan hosts Kyoto conference on climate change.	**1994** Channel tunnel opened. **1999** NATO intervention in Kosovo.	**1993** Bill Clinton becomes US President. **1994** Nelson Mandela elected President of South Africa.
2001 Junichiro becomes Prime Minister vowing to clean up politics and restore economic growth. **2002** Japan co-hosts soccer World Cup.	**2002** Euro currency comes into use.	**200** George W. Bush becomes US President. **2001** Terrorist attacks on New York and Washington D.C.

Glossary

A

archaeologist: a person who studies the past by **excavating** ancient sites.

archipelago: a group of islands

armourer: a person who makes or mends arms, such as guns, and armour.

assassinate: to murder someone, usually a political figure.

atomic bomb: a type of bomb that is powered by a nuclear reaction.

B

beach: to run or haul a ship up on to a beach or shore.

Buddhism: a religion begun by the Indian Gautama about 2,500 years ago. He said that by destroying greed and hatred, which are the causes of suffering, people may reach **enlightenment**.

C

calligraphy: the art of beautiful handwriting.

census: an official count of the population which includes such information as people's age and occupation.

Confucius: a Chinese philosopher who lived about 551–479 BCE. He taught virtue and responsibility and that everyone had their own place in society.

conscript: a person who is forced to sign up for military service.

constitution: the basic laws by which a state or nation is governed.

consul: an official who is appointed by his or her country to protect its business interests and look after its citizens in a foreign country.

convert: to cause someone to change their beliefs.

council: a group of people who have been elected or appointed to oversee administration and law.

cremate: to burn a dead body.

D

daimyo: important Japanese landowners who became warlords, making war against their neighbours.

diplomat: an official who negotiates for his or her country in a foreign country.

disciples: followers of particular leaders or teachings.

drill: in military terms, the training of soldiers in procedures such as the use of weapons.

E

economics: the study of finances and businesses.

embassy: the residence or place of business for any foreign official in a specific country.

enlightened: to have seen the light or truth of the matter.

excavate: to dig up in a methodical and scientific manner.

exports: goods that are sold abroad.

F

fortifications: especially strong defences around cities or castles.

G

glacier: a slowing moving mass of ice.

governor: a senior administrator of a society.

guilds: an association of people, such as merchants, with the same interests.

I

imports: goods that are bought into a country from abroad.

investment: the act of putting money into projects.

J

Jesuit: a member of a Roman Catholic order. The order of the Jesuits was set up by Ignatius Loyola in 1534 to defend Catholicism against reform.

junk: a Chinese boat.

K

kimono: a loose-sashed, ankle-length garment with wide sleeves.

Kublai Khan: (c.1215–94), ruler of China and Mongolia, and grandson of Genghis Khan.

L

lacquer: a hard glossy coating on decorative objects.

M

migrate: to go from one place to settle in another.

missionaries: people who try to **convert** others to their religion.

Mongols: people who come from Mongolia in Central Asia.

O

occupation: the period of Japanese history after the Second World War when American forces lived in Japan.

P

persecute: to treat others badly because of their race or religion.

pronunciation: the way to say particular sounds.

province: an area ruled as a part of a country or state.

puppet-state: a country that seems independent but is in fact controlled by another.

R

reforms: improvements made to existing rules and customs.

S

samurai: the Japanese warrior class that started in the 11th century. Samurai were prepared to fight and die for their **daimyos**, to whom they swore undying loyalty.

Shinto: the ancient Japanese religion meaning 'the way of the gods'. Its followers believed in spirits called *kami* lived in gods, nature and the emperor.

shogun: a title given to a warlord meaning 'great barbarian-conquering supreme general'. Shoguns always came from the warrior class of the samurai.

survey: to plot a detailed view of an area of land.

T

taxes: an amount of money that everyone has to pay to the government.

treaty: a formal agreement between two or more states.

V

vaccination: a method of enabling people to resist dangerous diseases.

Index

Numbers in **bold** indicate an illustration. Words in **bold** are in the glossary on page 47.

This edition published in 2003 by
Belitha Press
A member of Chrysalis Books plc
64 Brewery Road, London N7 9NT

Copyright © in this format Belitha Press
Illustrations copyright © Robina Green
Text copyright © Richard Tames

ISBN 1 84138 652 9

Typeset by Chambers Wallace, London

Printed in Hong Kong

British Library Cataloguing in Publication Data for this book is available from the British Library.

Editor: Kate Scarborough
Designer: Simon Borrough
Picture researcher: Juliet Duff
Series Consultant: Shane Winser, Royal Geographical Society, London
Consultant: Akiko Motoyoshi

Photographic credits

Ancient Art and Architecture Collection: 11 top, 18 bottom, 28 left, 29 top.
Asahi Shimbun Photos, Tokyo: 29 bottom.
Bridgeman Art Library: 14 bottom, Tokugawa Reimeikai Foundation, Tokyo; 23 bottom Private Collection, 37 bottom Giraudon/Musee d'Orsay, Paris.
Comstock Photos: 9 bottom left.
ET Archive: 8 centre Freer Gallery of Art; 22, 30 bottom British Museum; 35 Postal Museum, Frankfurt; 36 top right Private Collection; 38 top, 39 top, 41 top.
Mary Evans Picture Library: 34 top, 36 centre, 40 bottom.
Werner Forman Archive: title page; 2, 3 National Museum, Kyoto; 7 left Private Collection; 10, 11 bottom, 13 top; 21 bottom British Museum; 24 bottom Kuroda Collection Japan; 25 bottom Tempus Collection, London; 27 top Basho Kenshokai, Ueno.
Fukuzawa Memorial Centre for Modern Japanese Studies, Keio University: 32 top.
Robert Harding Picture Library: 19 centre; 17 both, 32 bottom.
Michael Holford: endpapers, 9 top, 30-31.
Hulton Deutsch Collection: 24 top, 33, 34 bottom, 39 bottom.
Hutchison Library: 44 bottom, 45 bottom.
Images Colour Library: Cover right.
Japan Archive: 8 bottom, 15 both, 16 top, 21 top, 42.
Japan Information and Cultural Centre: 4, 44 top, 45 top.
Photri Inc: 41 bottom.
Popperfoto: 7 right, 36 top left, 43.
Rijksmuseum voor Volkenkunde, Leiden: 29 centre.
Tony Stone Worldwide: Front and back cover.
Richard Tames: 12 top, 16 bottom, 20, 23 top, 26 both, 27 bottom, 38 bottom.
Zefa Picture Library: 19 bottom.

This publication is supported by a grant from Tokio Marine Kagami Memorial Foundation through the Association for 100 Japanese Books.